Therese
Teacher of Prayer

by
Brother Craig

*All booklets are published thanks to the
generous support of the members of the
Catholic Truth Society*

CATHOLIC TRUTH SOCIETY
PUBLISHERS TO THE HOLY SEE

Contents

*To Mummy from whom
I learned of St Thérèse*

Learning from example

Some years ago when I told a renowned theologian that I was writing about St Thérèse as a Teacher of Prayer the response was that, "she did not write anything on prayer." But she did. What she wrote is perhaps over-shadowed by her doctrine of the Little Way and that the "other Teresa" - of Avila - wrote so much and so profoundly on prayer. It is true that not all we learn about prayer from St Thérèse come from her writing.[1] Much has comes from writings about her. That is, the lessons we learn about prayer by her example.

The secret, I believe, of St Thérèse's teaching on prayer is the same as her secret of sanctity. The shortest distance between two places is St Thérèse learning about a truth of the spiritual life and whole heartily put into action. She began this as a very young child and continued it throughout her life.

Regarding Prayer, she learned that prayer saved souls. So she prayed much for them. She prayed for the murderer Pranzzini. He was converted. She, still a child, asked a nun how to do mediation for she learned of its value. So she meditated. She learned the value of praying to our Heavenly Mother whom she loved greatly. So with tender devotion she prayed to Our Lady. As a Carmelite Nun before she began a task she would first pray to Our Lady.

St Thérèse was all for what are called 'devotions'. She prayed to the Infant Jesus and to the "Man of Sorrows" as shown on the image of the Holy Face. Like the foundress of the reform of the Carmelites, St Teresa of Avila, St Thérèse had a special devotion to St Joseph.

St Thérèse had a fervent love for the Blessed Sacrament and her favourite assignment as a nun was being sacristan. St Thérèse prayed for a logical reason (and this would help her when the devout feels no longer existed during her Dark Night of the Soul)[2] because she was a pragmatist. She prayed because it worked: it brought about results. It was effective. In writing to a missionary priest (Abbé Belliere, who had written requesting a nun to "adopt his ministry") St Thérèse wrote that she was happy to write to him but felt prayer and suffering were the best way to save souls.

For St Thérèse the spiritual life was simple. Others may make it complicated but not her. She prayed because she believed what the Church and her saints taught about prayer. It was as simple as that. May St Thérèse teach all of us the benefits and value of prayer and may we all let her be our teacher of prayer.

Brother Craig, St Joseph Monastery

Prayer in the life of St Thérèse before she became a Carmelite

To understand the prayer life of St Thérèse, or rather to understand St Thérèse, one must understand her home life. One must shed a tear over Mrs Martin's death, shake hands with dear Mr Louis Martin and be introduced to the Visitandine, Leonie, the devoted godmother, Marie, the little mother, Pauline and the other half of the Saint's soul, Céline. Today, when one visits Les Buissonnets (the name of the Saint's home in Lisieux) one can almost see the life that went on there - a life of prayer, work, study and recreation, all at their ordered times, a well-to-do, scheduled life completely free from worldliness. Thérèse, destined for a special mission in the Church, spent her early years in a very special family. The impression one receives is of the order that reigned in their household. This order tells us that they were united and in agreement as to their way of life. What was this way of life, first in the town of Alençon and then in Lisieux?

Family life

Thérèse was welcomed into this wonderful family on January 2, 1873. "On January 3, Marie-Francoise-Thérèse was baptized at the Church of Notre Dame. Her older sister Marie was the godmother, and the young son of a family friend, Paul-Albert Boul, was the godfather, both aged thirteen."[3] She was loved by all, but to her father she was his queen. At three years old St Thérèse began "attending" the lessons Marie would give Céline. She was an intelligent child and at this age she had already learned the alphabet. Soon she and Céline were counting their acts of self denial on a string of beads. She prayed and she and Céline talked about religion. On Sundays before Thérèse was old enough to attend Mass, she waited anxiously for Céline to return, bringing blessed bread. (It was a custom in France at the time to bring home bread that had been blessed). One cannot consider the piety of Thérèse as games that the children of devout families play. For it was at this early age that she dedicated herself to God. Years later the Saint told the Bishop of Bayeux that she had wished to give herself to God from the time she was three. Even more amazing is that she could say that from the age three she had never refused God anything!

Sorrow

But soon sorrow was to enter the life of Thérèse for the first time. Her mother died of cancer on August 28, 1877. From this time on Pauline was to become her "little mother." Two months later the Martins moved to Lisieux to be near their aunt and uncle and cousins. "Louis Martin was now forty-four years old. He had five little girls to raise, Alençon had always been his home but the family ties with Lisieux, less than fifty-five miles from rue Saint-Blaise [his street in Alençon] were very close."[4] Their uncle, Mrs Martin's brother, a dedicated Catholic, found them the perfect house, "Les Buissonnets". It was here that the prayer life and vocation of Thérèse was to develop.

After her mother's death, Thérèse became increasingly timid and shy. She was at peace only among her family. At home she would often speak about God and she was very devoted to Our Lady. She would never miss saying her prayers and was careful not to complain when blamed unjustly. Each afternoon her father would take her for a walk and they would make a visit to the Blessed Sacrament. This was how she first visited the Chapel of the Carmel. At eight she began her classes at the Benedictine Abbey school. She suffered greatly at school due to the jealousy of the other students. She had been put in a class ahead of her age. This, of course caused some of her classmates to resent her. During these trials her soul was developing as we can see from the fact that she didn't even tell her family about these school problems.

Thérèse was still quite young when Céline made her First Holy Communion. She decided, with her characteristic determination, to begin her preparation then also. She argued that four years was surely not too much time to prepare to receive Our Eucharistic Lord. She even determined to start a new life at Céline's First Holy Communion.

Another sorrow entered Thérèse's life when Pauline, her "little mother" told her she would soon be entering Carmel. "Pauline at once explained the meaning of the Carmelite life. The child of nine years listened avidly: this life of Jesus alone, attracted her.[5] When Pauline described the life of the Carmelite Nuns to her little sister, the Saint realized that this was her vocation also. She was certain that her desire to enter Carmel was from God and not because of Pauline.

After Pauline entered Carmel, Thérèse became very ill. Some consider the loss of her "little mother" the cause of her illness. Yet the Saint herself declared that her illness was caused by the devil in revenge for the harm her family was going to do to him. Thérèse was very ill and her family was very concerned. Her father especially was suffering, as nothing seemed to cure her. Mr Martin asked for Masses to be said at the Shrine of Our Lady of Victories in Paris. It was during this Novena of Masses that Our Lady cured Thérèse. This we shall consider later.

First Holy Communion

Thérèse was cured and her sickness never again returned. Fully recovered, she began to prepare for her First Holy Communion. During this time she experienced great peace, all disquietude left her soul. It was Marie who gave her the instructions in preparation, teaching her the value of "Little things" and teaching her about renunciation, which became a favourite subject of the Saint's thoughts.

At this time in the life of the Saint she began to do mental prayer or meditation. She had a great interest in prayer. She asked an older pupil how to meditate. Once, one of the nuns asked her what she did at home. She told the nun that she often hid in a corner of her room where she could shut herself off with the bed curtains. There she thought about God, about the shortness of life, about eternity. Later she realized that this was mental prayer guided by God.

Thérèse benefited greatly from the retreat she made at the Abbey before her First Holy Communion. "The instructions were given by Father Domin, who had been chaplain of the Benedictine school for forty-one years."[6] She was especially inspired by a holy card Céline sent her of a small flower at the door of the Tabernacle. Thérèse describes the graces she received at the moment of her First Holy Communion. "I knew that I was loved and I, in my turn, told Him that I loved Him, and was giving myself to Him for all eternity. There were no demands made of me, no sacrifices; it has been years that we had been exchanging looks, He and I, insignificant though I was, we understood each other.

And now it wasn't a question of looks, something had melted away, and there were no longer two of us, Thérèse had simply disappeared, like a drop in the ocean; Jesus only was left, my Master, my King. Hadn't I begged Him to take away my liberty, because I was so afraid of the use I might make of it; hadn't I longed, weak and helpless as I was, to be united once and for all with that Divine Strength."[7]

These are not the words of an ordinary child; these are the words of a child who already understands the spiritual life and the way of prayer. Already the "Little Flower" had determined her life and had totally consecrated her life to God. She already understood the mystery of the Holy Eucharist, that we are transformed into the Lord whom we receive.

On the afternoon of her First Holy Communion day, Thérèse was chosen to read the Act of Consecration to Our Lady. She said she gave herself to Our Lady "like a child throwing its arms around its mother and asking for her protection".[8] After her First Holy Communion she greatly desired to receive the Holy Eucharist. From then on Our Lord alone could fill her heart. She longed for the moment when she could receive Him again. She received permission to receive Holy Communion on all the great feasts. It was after receiving Holy Communion, at this time in her life, that Thérèse received a great desire for suffering.

Soon after, she was confirmed. She tells us in her autobiography, "My experience when the Holy Spirit came to me was not that of a strong wind blowing; it was more like that 'whisper of a gentle breeze.' which Elias heard on Mount Horeb."[9]

Scruples and sensitivity

A year after her First Holy Communion Thérèse made a retreat. It was then that she began to be plagued by scruples. About this time Marie entered Carmel and Thérèse realized that life with so many partings and sorrows isn't where one will find enjoyment. She was particularly saddened by the fact that Marie could no longer help her with her problem of scruples, as this sister advised her about what to confess and what to ignore as a scruple. Thérèse's family had lost two sisters and two brothers before she was born. They died as babies yet were not forgotten by the family. She turned to them in prayer and her scruples were instantly cured.

Another cure was awaiting Thérèse. Since the age of four she was very sensitive. Now she was fourteen. One Christmas Eve, after Midnight Mass, she overheard her father, who was tired, remark that he was glad that this would be the last year they would have to fill Thérèse's boots with presents. Céline looked at Thérèse knowing that this was enough to cause many tears and advised her to wait to open her presents. But no, this was a different

Thérèse. She went and opened her presents cheerfully as if she hadn't heard. Her father, whose good humor had returned, was delighted. (These "moods" the family was to later realize were simply the beginning of his serious illness.) Thérèse tells us herself that she had received this special grace, this special cure from the Infant Jesus on Christmas Eve. She says that she "had recovered the strength of mind which she'd lost at four and a half and recovered it for good."[10]

Prayer for souls

A great increase of charity entered the soul of Thérèse at this time. She immediately began her apostolate. She began to pray for the salvation of souls. She wanted to save them from Hell. At Mass one Sunday a holy card moved somewhat out from her missal. Thérèse noticed a picture of the Crucifixion. She was struck by the sight of the Precious Blood flowing from one of the hands of Jesus. She thought, "How pitiful that It should be allowed to fall on the ground unheeded, instead of being jealously hoarded up! I would take up my stand, at the foot of the Cross, and gather up this Saving Balm with the intention of applying it to the needs of souls. The cry of Our Blessed Lord on the Cross, 'I Thirst' went on echoing in me; and this kindled in me a zeal which I'd never known before - how could I allay His thirst for souls except by sharing It?"[11]

In this prayer we find the complete plan of the vocation of Thérèse; reparation and salvation. Her intention was to save the Precious Blood from being lost and then she would contemplate the Crucifixion and by prayer bring the grace of the Redemption to others. She, like her Holy Mother St Teresa of Avila, would be a contemplative and an apostle, or rather, a contemplative apostle.

She prayed for a murderer named Pranzzini and asked for a sign. Both his conversion and the sign were granted. Right before his execution he took the priest's crucifix and kissed the Five Wounds. This encouraged the Saint in her apostolate of prayer.

During this time Thérèse did a great deal of spiritual reading. Even before she made her First Holy Communion she had read "*The Imitation of Christ*." She knew it as if by heart. At fourteen years old she read Father Arminjon's, "*The End of The Present Time and the Mysteries of The Future Life*." This book made a great impression on her and was a great influence on her prayer life. She tells us in her autobiography, "all the tremendous truths of religion, all mysteries of eternity, came flooding into my soul with a feeling of happiness that had nothing to do with the world. I was getting a foretaste, already, of the welcome God has prepared for those who love Him. Yes, hearts can feel what eye has never seen; and realizing that there is no proportion between those heavenly rewards and the little sacrifices we make in this life, I longed to love Our Lord, love Him passionately, show Him, while life still offered its unique chance, a thousand proofs of my love."[12]

Quest for holiness

The prayers of Thérèse were very much concerned with the meaning of this life and the reality of Heaven. For heaven was very real to her. It was often the subject of her thoughts and prayers. It was the first word she wrote as a child. Later Heaven was to be the "subject" of her trial of faith. Yet, for now, all was light and prayerful consideration.

Thérèse and her sister Céline had very special spiritual conversations by a large window in a room on the third floor at "Les Buissonnets" and these conversations reminded them of the 'Conversations' of St Augustine and St Monica at Ostia which St Augustine wrote of in his book *"The Confessions."* Thérèse tells us that she and Céline received great graces at this time. Holiness seemed easy to them and they set out to achieve it.

There existed a very special friendship between Thérèse and her sister Céline. They were united in their quest for holiness. Both were devoted to the martyrs whose lives they had read and from this reading and discussing their heroic lines they received a great influence to their spirituality. Like the martyrs before execution, they would encourage one another in the way of prayer and perfection. Later they would write very special letters to each other and encourage one another in their vocations and especially in their apostolate of prayer for sinners and in praying for priests.

These conversations and this special friendship encouraged the prayer life of Thérèse. Some time before, she had asked a Benedictine, Sister Henriette, about mental prayer. She replied that she talked to God as a father, that she spoke to Him of her joys and her sorrows, and that she made mental prayer with the heart. Thérèse liked the good nun's answer.

Prayer from the heart

The prayer of Thérèse was surely "with the heart". Her prayer at this time and throughout her entire life was from the heart. Her prayer was conversational. She simply spoke to God, Our Lady and the saints. She talked as a child speaks to its mother and father. Even before she entered Carmel she received very special graces of prayer and sometimes experienced a great ardor. Although Thérèse was favoured with extraordinary graces at times, normally she "walked" in faith.

It was at this time that her love reached the height of folly and she prayed to be able to go into Hell so that someone there would love God. She knew that this wasn't to be, yet she knew that love had inspired this prayer.

Although there was ardor and consolation in the prayer of Thérèse, we also find much dryness and aridity. Later this dryness will be the "state" of her prayer. Even before she entered Carmel she experienced a feeling of "dryness" in prayer often referred to as "aridity."

At the age of fifteen Thérèse began to seek entrance into Carmel. She believed that it was God's will that she should enter soon and at such a young age. Her requests to the Bishop and His Holiness Pope Leo XIII are famous. During these painful and daring experiences she suffered from aridity in prayer and a feeling of "abandonment." Yet she was peaceful and had the certainty she was doing God's will.

As we know, before "traveling" to Carmel the Saint was to travel to Rome. She was very pleased to visit Italy and Rome. She enjoyed Rome with its memories of the martyrs, saw the shrines of St Anthony in Padua, St Catherine, the Poor Clare Abbess, in Bologna and St Mary Magdalene de Pazzi, the great Carmelite mystic in Florence. Especially did she cherish the memory of receiving Holy Communion in the home of the Holy Family at Loreto.

After she returned home she finally received permission to enter Carmel. She was told, however, that she could not enter until after Lent. During this delay she dedicated herself to an even more mortified life. She carefully explained what she meant by mortification. She did not mean severe penances but the denial of her will and finding many opportunities for little acts of penance or mortification.

Prayer in the life of St Thérèse
as a Carmelite

Regarding her becoming a Carmelite, Thérèse stated that she was there to save souls and to pray for priests. She felt she should do this by suffering. The more she suffered the more she was attracted to it. Of course, prayer would give her the strength to suffer.

Since the life of a contemplative is a life of prayer and penance, in order to understand the prayer of Thérèse let us consider her penances and spirit of mortification. Before she entered Carmel she denied her will and did little penances or acts of mortification. In Carmel she spoke against extraordinary penances as not her way. Yet the penances and austerity she accepted and desired were quite great. She took the discipline (a little whip or scourge used to strike one's shoulders and back) and when it was discussed she said she wanted to feel as much pain as possible. She then "went on to tell Céline that although tears often came to her eyes she forced herself to smile in order, as she said, that her face might express the feelings of her heart - delight at suffering in unison with Jesus."[13]

Hardships

In Carmel Thérèse had much to suffer. Without complaining she accepted poor food, poverty, work and most painful of all, the cold. Some nights she never slept, she simply shivered the entire night. Her hands were covered with chilblains. In the summer she worked in an airless part of the laundry and this was by her own choice. Whenever she was mistreated, whether it was water accidentally splashed in her face in the laundry or the impatience of an elderly and sickly nun, she never complained. To this she added many hidden acts of self-denial that completely conquered her self-will and allowed God's will to reign in her, so much so, that during her last illness she could say that she had never done her own will.

It is necessary to understand that her prayer was coupled with a solid foundation of penance and mortification. Her prayer was one of a faithful soul, willing to carry her cross. Her prayer was the prayer of one who first accepted suffering, then desired it, then found peace and joy in suffering until she became a victim for reparation and the salvation of souls.

Dryness

From her first days in Carmel Thérèse had much to suffer. Not the least of her suffering was dryness and aridity in prayer. This was especially acute during her retreats. Before receiving the habit, she made a retreat that was "in the desert" of dryness. During this retreat she wrote to Pauline of dryness and said that she was plunged in darkness. Yet she was glad for this darkness if, in making an offering of it, she could console Jesus. She found consolation in looking at the image of the Holy Face of Jesus. She advised Céline to gaze at His Holy Face and see His glazed and sunken eyes. She told her sister that then she would see that He loves us.

When Thérèse experienced painful dryness she considered it a trial to detach her from all that was not Jesus. When she seemed so poor and had nothing to offer God in prayer she offered Him little "nothings." Following St Teresa of Avila, she taught that when we have no wood to get the fire of our love going we can still cast on this fire a few straws. These acts of good intention are very pleasing to God. Then God will place much wood on the fire. Thérèse tells us that she experienced this.

After she received the habit her spiritual dryness became even worse. It became, as she said, her "daily bread." Yet she was quite pleased since this way all her desires for suffering were fulfilled. Even after receiving Holy Communion she was in this state of aridity and at that time she had the least consolation. This trial of aridity was, according to Father Jarmart, O.C.D., the author of *"The Complete Spirituality of St Thérèse,"* part of the Saint's Dark Nights. At first, he tells us, she was tried regarding the virtue of charity and later there was a more painful trial of her faith and hope, the other theological virtues. This aridity, along with other sufferings, especially her father's illness, seems to have made up the 'Dark Night of the Senses' for the Saint.

State of prayer

Let us try to learn at what "stage" of prayer Thérèse was during these years in Carmel, at least until her Dark Night of the Soul began. Later we shall consider her "offering" which was made during these years of dryness yet before the trial of faith began. Of course, it is not easy to state the stage of a soul's prayer and spiritual progress especially since we do not find in the Saint's writings a step-by-step description of her stages of prayer. We can guess that God lifted her to higher stages of prayer rather early in life.

Thérèse indicates by what she tells us about her prayer that from even before her entrance into Carmel and, surely during her first years there, she enjoyed what is called the Prayer of Simplicity, the prayer of Simple Regard, or rather the prayer of the awareness of the Presence of God. Thérèse simply spoke to God and lived in a state of prayer. She prayed with confidence and love. Her prayer was a look of love, a gaze of adoration. Much of her prayer is of this nature. Later there will be what is called Ecstatic Prayer and then she will reach the heights of the Transforming Union. Yet even then her prayer has this characteristic of a conversation, of a gaze of love, of a child who allows its father to carry it.

Presence of God

Therefore, it seems that Thérèse lived constantly with an awareness of the Presence of God, not a "felt" awareness but rather one of faith and love. There is no indication in any of the Saint's writings that she read the treatise of Brother Lawrence of the Resurrection, a French Carmelite who died in 1691: "*Practice of The Presence of God*" about the awareness of the Presence of God. It would seem though, that as a Carmelite, she would have read it. What is undeniable is that she lived this doctrine. Throughout her life she lived in a state of recollection. As the other French Carmelite nun, Blessed Elizabeth of the Blessed Trinity, lived adoring the Blessed Trinity within her, her "sister," St Thérèse, lived with an awareness of being a child carried by God. Her heart and mind were constantly turned to God. This explains her statement that she had never gone three minutes without thinking of God. One of the other nuns once told the Saint that she was, as it were, "possessed" by God.

The Dark Night of the Soul

When her Dark Night of the Soul began Thérèse simply advanced along her spiritual journey. In darkness she continued to believe, pray, hope and live, aware of God.

When God seemed to be hidden from her she never prayed less, she prayed even more. She preferred the darkness of faith, offering what she suffered so others could be given light. The Saint wrote that the clouds might cover the sun, yet not only does she not doubt the sun's existence, she continues to look, with a simple gaze of love, in the direction of the sun. She explains this to her sister Marie in a way that shows once again her great literary ability. Thérèse considers herself a "little bird" that has learned to look at the Sun (God) like the Eagles (the saints). She says she remains keeping her eyes fixed looking at the Sun, "deterred by no obstacle, storm and rain cloud-wrack may conceal its heavenly radiance, but I don't shift my view - I know that it is there all the time behind the clouds, its brightness never dimmed. Sometimes, to be sure, the storm thunders at my heart; I find it difficult to believe in the existence of anything except the clouds which limit my horizon. It's only then that I realize the possibilities of my weakness; find consolation in staying at my post and directing my gaze toward one invisible light which communicates itself, now only to the eye of faith."[14]

The Saint understood her experience very well to be able to explain it so well. The above quotation from her letter to her sister Marie, which forms part of her autobiography, teaches that her "way of prayer" was essentially a gaze of love.

Thérèse, like a little child, spoke to God, listened to God, simply enjoyed being in the Presence of God and with love, gazed at God. This way of prayer developed until she reached the height of the Transforming Union. Yet before reaching this height the Saint was to enter the Dark Night, the Night of Faith.

Complete darkness

Here we are considering what the theologians call, "The Dark Night of The Soul." It seems to occur when the person leaves what is called the "Illuminative Way" and is about to enter the "Unitive Way." This Unitive Way is a name theologians give to the heights of holiness where the person is totally united to God. We know that the Saint said that this trial began just when she could suffer it. Sooner and she would, she said, not have been able to suffer this great trial. Her trial of faith, or Dark Night of the Soul seems to have begun instantly and the Saint was sure, right away, that it would last a long time. What was this darkness like? She told the prioress, Mother Marie de Gonzague, that if she wished to understand her trial she must imagine that she (Thérèse) had been born in a country covered with a very thick mist; had never seen nature in her "smiling mood," but had heard of all these experiences ever since childhood and knew that the country in which she lived is not her native country. Yet her country cannot be seen. There is complete darkness.

To understand how painful this trial was to Thérèse we must remember how much Heaven meant to her and how, before the Dark Night, she could easily think about Heaven. The darkness was all around her, complete, as she said, yet she tells us there was no darkness in her devotion to Our Blessed Mother.

In this trial she continued to be faithful and continued to believe. She tells us that she made more acts of faith during this time than during her whole life. She even wrote beautiful poems about Heaven, of what she "willed" to believe. She even said that her soul was blindfolded. There were rays of light, yet afterwards the darkness was blacker than ever, especially during her last illness. The darkness took on the voice of "the unbeliever" to disturb her, telling her that the "land of Light she believed in didn't exist and that death would bring a greater darkness. The devil also tried to disturb her. She asked for a blessed candle and holy water.

What was the purpose of this trial?

It seems to have been twofold; first, to perfect the Saint and secondly, for an apostolic purpose - that by the blackness she suffered, unbelievers would receive light. The Saint was quite conscious of both aspects. Of the first she said that her desire for Heaven was being perfected, that all that was "natural" in it was being removed. She also understood that this trial had an apostolic value - to give light to others. She offered her trial for this intention. She continued heroically to pray and faithfully live the Carmelite life during this trial which was to last until her last agony. She made acts of faith, prayed, showed great charity to others, great patience in her illness and even continued to find ways to practice mortification. She thought of others and not of herself. She continued her prayers and penances for missionaries. During this time the Saint did not pray less, she prayed more. She never omitted the two hours of mental prayer the nuns did each day, the praying of the Liturgy of the Hours and she continued her fervent prayers throughout the day. When prayer was especially difficult she would recite one "Our Father" or a "Hail Mary" for she said the prayers ravish her, they nourished her soul with a divine food. In the dryness of the desert, Thérèse continued to pray.

St Thérèse's last illness

During the night of Good Friday, 1897, Thérèse received the first warning of her last illness. As she laid down on her cot, blood rushed to her mouth. The next morning she looked at her handkerchief and saw that it was filled with blood. In May she was freed from all her duties. in July she was taken to the infirmary. In August she received Holy Viaticum. Through September she suffered greatly until on the 30th of September she died. During these months she suffered terribly from consumption, suffocation and, perhaps especially, from the treatment of cauterization. During this illness she suffered from privation regarding the reception of Holy Communion. She also suffered greatly from her trial of faith. Yet through these months with her heroic abandonment to the will of God Thérèse continued to progress in the way of perfection and the way of prayer.

During these months of illness she not only prayed, she asked her sisters to pray for her. She asked that they pray not for healing but for strength to suffer. St Bernadette had made this same request. Thérèse even prayed that the good of her medicines which she took in obedience would be applied not to her but to missionaries. The Saint continued to pray for others. When her sisters were working in the laundry, in the heat of the summer, she prayed that God would console them and that they would work in love and peace.

One can learn a great deal about prayer from the example of the prayer of Thérèse during her last illness. Important statements about prayer made by Thérèse during her last illness are found in a notebook kept by Céline who wrote; "I arose several times during the night in spite of her objections. On one of these visits I saw my dear little sister with hands joined and eyes raised to Heaven 'What are you doing? You should be sleeping.' I said. She answered by saying, 'I can't sleep, I'm suffering too much so I'm praying.' Then I asked what do you say to Jesus? She answered, 'I say nothing, I love Him.'"[15]

Here we can see that the loving gaze of Thérèse has simplified even further. In the development of her prayer life we see that the gaze of love has simply become love. It is no longer looking with love. It is simply to love. Here we see the perfection of the mystical life and the spiritual life; the perfection of charity. Now for Thérèse it is no longer a question of "praying." It is a question of love. Now her soul is transformed completely into an act of love. Words aren't necessary anymore, just love. Love will speak, love will pray.

My God, I love you

During her last agony, on 30th September, suffering greatly and still in the Dark Night of the Soul, the Saint uttered many fervent prayers of love. She prayed much to Our Blessed Mother. In the afternoon her sisters were moving her slightly, her arms were outstretched like a cross. The clock struck; it was three o'clock. At six o'clock the Angelus rang. Thérèse looked at the statue of Our Lady. Céline put some ice on her lips and Thérèse gave her a very special look, a look that said to Céline, "Go, I will be with you." Then a few minutes past seven she asked the Mother Prioress if she was experiencing the last agony. When told yes but that it may continue for a few more hours she answered, "Well, all right, all right. Oh, I wouldn't want to suffer for a shorter time!" Looking at her crucifix, she said, "Oh, I love Him. My God, I love

You!"[16] With this last prayer of love uttered still in the Dark Night of the Soul she spoke her last words, her last act of love. Then for a moment or two, the space of a Credo, her sisters saw that she was no longer aware of them. She was in ecstasy. In this ecstasy she died. Yet it was when she was still in the Dark Night that she uttered her last prayer of love, "My God, I love You."

St Thérèse's Act of Oblation

One of the most significant aspects of the prayer of
Thérèse is her "Act of Oblation to The Merciful Love of
God." From the beginning it is best to understand that
the offering she made on the Feast of The Most Blessed
Trinity was an offering to accept the Merciful Love of
God - it was not an offering to suffer. The "Little
Flower" surely was a real victim soul, a soul dedicated to
suffering in reparation for sin and for the salvation of
souls. Yet this is not what she is expressing in her
"Oblation."

During the Mass of the Feast of the Most Blessed
Trinity, Thérèse realized how much Our Saviour, Jesus
Christ wishes to bestow His love on souls and that there
were very few to accept this love. After receiving
permission from the Prioress, she and her sister Céline,
kneeling before the statue of Virgin of the Smile and
recited their offering.

Thérèse wrote down the prayer and kept it in her book
of the Gospels. Her offering begins with an act of love to
the Most Blessed Trinity and her desire to save souls, to
deliver souls from Purgatory and to work for the
glorification of the Church. She then expresses her desire

to fulfill God's will perfectly and reach the exact degree of glory God has willed for her.

She expresses her desire to be a saint. Since she believes that she is not able to be a saint on her own she asks for God's holiness. She then recalls that the Infinite Merits of Jesus are hers and she asks God to look at her through the eyes of Jesus, to look at her in the Sacred Heart of Jesus. She then offers the merits of the Blessed Virgin Mary and of the saints and holy angels to God. She asks Our Lady to present her oblation to God. She expresses her desires with confidence. She asks that God take possession of her soul. She notes that she cannot receive Holy Communion as often as she would like so she asks that the Blessed Sacrament remain in her heart as in a tabernacle, between each of her receptions of Holy Communion.

She then expresses her desire to console God by reparation because so few are grateful. She prays that God will take away her freedom which may cause her to displease Him. She adds that if she falls through weakness she asks God to heal and cure her of this fault instantly by His loving gaze. She then thanks God for all the graces she has received. She is especially thankful for having passed through the "crucible of suffering." She then states that "It is with joy that I shall look upon You on the last day, bearing the scepter of the Cross, since You have deigned to give me that most precious Cross as my portion. I hope to be like You in Heaven and see the Sacred Stigmata of Your Passion in my body."[17]

She expresses her hope for Heaven yet professes that she is not working for merit but solely for love of God. Solely, she says to console "Your Sacred Heart and to save souls which will love You everlastingly."[18] She says that, at the end of her life, she will appear without any merits; she, therefore, desires to be given God's own justice and she trusts that in a single instant God can transform and perfect her soul. Now she expresses the actual offering. "To live in an act of perfect Love, I offer myself as a burnt offering to Your Merciful Love, calling you to consume me at every instant, while You let the floods of infinite tenderness within You flow into my soul, that so I may become a martyr to Your Love, O My God! ...When that martyrdom has prepared me to appear before You, may it cause me to die and my soul hurl itself in that one instant into the eternal embrace of Your Merciful Love. At every heartbeat, O my Beloved, I wish to renew this offering an infinite number of times till the shadows retire and I can tell You of my love over and over again, looking upon Your face to face eternally."[19]

Truly this offering is essentially an act of love by one who realized her vocation is love. It is interesting to note that the last words of this offering tell us a great deal about prayer, for eternity she wishes to tell God of her love.

Graces of prayer

That Thérèse's spiritual life was without extraordinary phenomena compared to other saints has been stated by authors quite often. This basically is correct if we understand that what is meant is that "compared to other saints" she did not experience many of the mystical phenomena they experienced and that her way of spirituality is a way that does not exclude, yet does not "require," extraordinary graces. Yet, it must also be remembered that there were some extraordinary graces in her life.

The first extraordinary grace in the life of Thérèse was the vision she had as a child of her father's future illness when she saw a man in their yard, with his face covered, who then disappeared. And she was miraculously cured when she saw Our Lady smile. During prayer she received other special graces. Even before she entered Carmel she experienced, she tells us, while she prayed on summer evenings, the flights of the spirit described by St Teresa of Avila. This, of course, is a very extraordinary grace.

As a Carmelite she received similar graces. In 1889, while praying in the grotto of St Mary Magdalene, she was blessed with a state of what is called "Quietude" which lasted for a week. She described this by saying that something like a veil had been put over earthly things. She knew it was a supernatural state and found it difficult to describe. In keeping with Carmelite tradition the Saint refers to this grace as "mystical," that is, caused by the Holy Spirit and not by her own doing. She understood that the purpose of this grace was to make her more detached.

On the Friday after her Act of Oblation, she received a very extraordinary grace, the "wound of love." She was praying the Stations of the Cross when she felt pierced as it were by a dart of fire. This experience was so ardent that she thought she would die. She couldn't explain it. She felt plunged in fire, a fire full of sweetness. This lasted only a moment. Then she returned to her state of aridity. St John of the Cross in "*The Living Flame of Love*" teaches that not many souls are granted this favour. God gives it mainly to those who have followers. To these followers they transmit their virtue and spirit. Surely she was to have many followers of her Little Way!

Another grace of prayer she received was that, very often, she would receive inspirations or, as she called them: "lights." These lights were about understanding Sacred Scripture or the spiritual life. She said also that God inspired her, with what to say and do, she received these lights just when she needed them. They were especially helpful in instructing the novices. During the last months of her life these lights which inspired her were even prophetic. During this time she made many prophetic statements regarding her mission, her autobiography, the shower of roses and that she would be a saint!

The transforming union

Before considering if Thérèse reached this height of the spiritual life - the Transforming Union or the Mystical Marriage - let us consider this special grace.

Father Juan Arintero, O.P. tells us that the "holy person in this state is now dead to self, it lives only for God. Having lost self completely, it is despoiled of everything earthly and human and is clothed in the heavenly and the divine."[20]

It must be remembered, as Father Marie Eugene, O.C.D. states in his excellent work about the doctrine of St Teresa of Avila, "*I Am A Daughter of The Church*", that "perfect conformity with the will of God is the essential effect and practical criterion of perfect union."[21] The person who has been transformed lives only to do God's Will. The person, therefore, completely forgets himself or herself. Dom Vitalis Lehodey, O.C.S.O. says that these people forget their own interests and consider only those of God. Having reached this state Blessed Mary of Jesus Crucified, foundress of the Bethlehem Carmel, prayed in ecstasy "My God, I abandon myself to all Thou willest for me."[22] In this state of Transforming Union, the person is, as it were, "deified." When Teresa Helena Higginson (the English mystic and apostle of devotion to the Sacred Head of Jesus and to His Divine Intellect) reached this height of the Transforming Union and lived for seventeen years in this extraordinary state. She struggled to describe this grace and she quoted the words of St Paul, "Christ now liveth in me." Then she added that "as the soul is the life of the body so, and more truly, is Jesus the life of my soul. I am one with Him more closely than words can convey."[23]

St John of the Cross teaches that God reveals to these holy people, who have been transformed, the greatness of their virtues and the graces He has given them. "The person then conscious of the abundance of its enrichments knows that it is pure, rich, full of virtues and prepared for the Kingdom of God. God permits it, in this state, to discern its beauty and He entrusts to it the gifts and virtues He has bestowed, for everything is converted into love and praises, and it has no touch of presumption or vanity, since it no longer bears the leaven of imperfection which corrupts."[24] Not only does the person realize his or her virtues, he or she is also very much aware that he or she has been transformed and if this person has studied spiritual theology then he or she may even be aware that he or she has reached the Transforming Union. St Teresa of Avila confirms this teaching by stating that "Our Good God now desires to remove the scales from the eyes of the person so that it may see and understand something of the favour which He is granting her."[25]

Father Jamart, who has carefully studied the prayer of St Thérèse, believes that she did reach the Transforming Union. He writes, "Everything points to this fact. she suffered passive purgations [the Dark Nights] she was favoured with special graces of mental prayer that prepare for such a union, and she enjoyed the fruits of such a union"[26]

Thérèse tells us that from the time of her Oblation to the Merciful Love of God love completely surrounded her and permeated her soul, that this love renewed her and also purified her at every minute and had left not even a trace of sin in her. She had great peace and a great desire to suffer. Yet most of all she had great abandonment to the will of God. She tells us that she learned from experience that within us is the Kingdom of God and that Jesus, hidden in the bottom of her heart was surely acting within her.

Perhaps the most convincing sign of the Transforming Union in the life of Thérèse remembering the doctrine of St John of the Cross and St Teresa of Avila, is that she stated that no praise could cause even a shadow of vanity, that she understood humility and that she was a saint. God allowed her to be aware of her virtues and also her mission. This would not cause vanity because she was already transformed.

Some may claim that the "Little Flower" could not have reached the Transforming Union since she still suffered The Dark Night of the Soul which in her case was a trial of faith regarding the existence of Heaven. And, they argue, in the Transforming Union there are not these sufferings and trials. Yet both St Teresa of Avila and St John of the Cross state that ordinarily these souls no longer suffer, but there can be exceptions. St Teresa of Avila refers here to Our Lady and also St Paul because they had reached the Transforming Union and still suffered. Father Jamart considers St Theresa Margaret Reiti, the Italian Carmelite, someone who suffered even after reaching the Transforming Union. And we must also remember the apostolic purpose of the trial of Thérèse, that her darkness would give light to others.

Particular devotions of St Thérèse

To the Virgin Mary

Since Thérèse was a member of the order of Our Lady of Mount Carmel I'll begin considering her devotions by discussing her Marian devotion. Thérèse was, throughout her entire life, a child of Mary. Let us consider now the special character of her devotion to Our Blessed Mother. She was especially devoted to Our Lady as the Mother of Jesus during His hidden years at Nazareth. She liked to contemplate the simplicity, poverty and prayerfulness of the Holy Family. In this the Saint was completely faithful to the Carmelite tradition. For the town of Nazareth is not far from the mountain of Carmel and the Carmelite life is a hidden life of prayer and work.

As a very small child she had great devotion to Our Lady. In the first essay she ever wrote she told of the Blessed Virgin Mary going to the temple as a child that she was remarkable among her companions for her piety and for her angelic sweetness. She related how everyone loved the child Mary, especially the angels, who regarded her as their little sister. She explained that she herself wanted to be a very good girl, that Our Lady was her dear Mother and that children usually resemble their mother.

After Pauline entered Carmel little Thérèse became very ill. She was delirious and suffering from hallucinations. One day during a severe crisis Marie knelt in prayer before a statue of Our Lady in Thérèse's sick room. Leonie and Céline joined in prayer Thérèse too, understandingly, turned toward the statue. She prayed with all her heart to her Mother in heaven, that she would have pity on her. All at once, Thérèse tells us, she saw the Virgin Mary smile upon her. She was instantly cured. The statue, from then on, became known as the Virgin of the Smile. Thérèse was to have this statue with her in the Carmel. Today it is above her remains in her shrine in the Carmelite chapel in Lisieux.

As mentioned earlier, on the day of Thérèse's First Holy Communion she was pleased to be chosen to recite the Act of Consecration to Our Lady. "That afternoon, it was I who recited the act of consecration to Our Lady; it was fitting that I, who had lost my earthly mother so young, should talk to my heavenly Mother in the name of the rest. And that is what I tried to do, talk to her; give myself up to her, like a child throwing its arms round its mother and asking for her protection I think she smiled down at me from Heaven, unseen; hadn't she smiled down visibly at me, and given life to the little flower that seemed to be fading away? And now she had brought her own Son to birth in me."[27]

Thérèse also sought entrance into the Sodality of the Children of Mary. "The Blessed Virgin, too, kept good watch over the little flower that was dedicated to her; she didn't want to see it tarnished with the stains of earth, so she took care to plant it high up, in her own mountain air, before it faded. That happy moment hadn't yet arrived, but already my love for my heavenly Mother was growing all the time; and I now went out of my way to prove. Soon after my first Communion I took a further step, and a new ribbon announced that I had become an 'aspirant' to fuller dedication as a Child of Mary; only I had to leave school before I actually joined the association And now, as I hadn't finished my schooling at the Abbey, I found I wasn't allowed to enter it on the strength of being an 'old girl.' That wouldn't have worried me much, only all my sisters had belonged, and I wanted to have the same right to call myself Our Lady's child as they had. So I pocketed my pride, and asked if I might join the Association at the Abbey. The headmistress didn't like to say no, but she made the condition that I must come round two afternoons in the week, so that they could judge whether I was worthy to be admitted... Well, if I went to the Abbey, it was only for Our Lady's sake. Sometimes I felt very lonely."[28]

After her pilgrimage to Paris and Rome her fondest memories were the visit to Our Lady of Victories in Paris and to the home of the Holy Family, the Holy House of

Loreto. "There was only one of them [the sights of Paris] that really took me out of myself and that was Notre Dame des Victoires. I can't describe what I felt, kneeling in front of the statue; I was so full of gratitude that it could only find its outlet (just as on my First Communion day) in tears. Our Lady gave me the assurance that she really had smiled at me, really had effected my cure; I knew that she really was watching over me, that I was her child - I began calling her 'Mamma,' because 'Mother' didn't seem intimate enough. Oh, I prayed so hard that she would go on looking after me and would make my dream come true before long by taking me under the protection of her stainless robe. I'd wanted that, from my earliest years and as I grew up I'd come to realize that, for me, Carmel was the only place where that shelter could be found."[29]

After entering the Carmelites Thérèse's devotion to Our Lady increased. The day the Church celebrates Our Lady's Nativity, 8th September, was chosen for the Saint's profession. She was very pleased about this choice.

She prayed that Our Lady would instruct her in the way of perfection. She prayed especially for inspiration in guiding the novices. She placed the statue of the Virgin of The Smile next to her cell, in a small oratory. Often she brought her novices there to counsel them, in the presence of Our Lady. She encouraged her missionary "brothers" (the two priests in the foreign missions whom she prayed for and encouraged with letters) to entrust their apostolate to Our Lady. Before beginning a task she would pray to Our Blessed Mother. She prayed before writing her autobiography that it would be written according to the wishes of Our Lady.

Thérèse said that to pray to the Mother of God is very special. She explained this by saying that when we pray to the saints they make us wait awhile, they have to go and present their requests to God. Yet when we pray for something, asking Our Lady to intercede for us - we do not have to wait. The Saint added that in her troubles and anxieties she quickly turned to the Virgin Mary - and she always helped her.

During her last illness, her devotion to Our Lady was especially fervent. She said she knew how greatly the Virgin Mary had suffered. She asked Our Blessed Mother how to benefit from her sufferings. One day she told a novice that she liked to hide her pains from God to give Him the impression that she was always glad. But hid nothing from Our Lady; to her, she told everything. When she was suffering from her trial of faith she prayed to Our Blessed Mother.

Regarding her last illness Thérèse prayed to Our Lady that little Thérèse would not be a burden to her sisters. One day Mother Agnes of Jesus (her sister Pauline) said death was distressing to those who had to look upon it. Thérèse spoke of Our Lady. She referred to how the

Blessed Virgin held Jesus, after he died, in her arms. He was covered with so many wounds. She marveled that Our Lady could endure such suffering.

When her suffering was very acute she turned to the statue of the Virgin of The Smile and prayed. She once said she could not pray but could only look at the Blessed Virgin Mary and say, "Jesus." Here we can see the spirituality of Thérèse. She looks at the statue of Our Blessed Mother and says the Holy Name of Jesus. In remembering Our Lady she does not forget Jesus and in remembering Jesus she does not forget Our Lady. For Thérèse it is simply Jesus and Mary.

One day she told her sister Pauline that she had prayed much to the Blessed Virgin during the night, thinking that Our Lady's wonderful month of May was about to begin.

During her last illness she turned to Our Lady. In the book known as the "*Last Conversations*" we read many Marian statements that the Saint made during these days of suffering. Several are quoted here.

"I asked the Blessed Virgin that I be not so tired and withdrawn as I have been all these days; I really felt that I was causing you pain. This evening she answered me."[30]

"I would, however, like to have a beautiful death to please you. I asked this from the Blessed Virgin. I didn't ask God for this because I want Him to do as He pleases. Asking the Blessed Virgin for something is not the same thing as asking God. She really knows what is to be done about my little desires, whether or not she must speak about them to God. So it's up to her to see that God is not forced to answer me, to allow Him to do everything He pleases."[31] And, "However, I do want to go! I've told the Blessed Virgin so and she can do what she pleases with my little wish."[32]

Thérèse believed that Our Lady who didn't have a Blessed Virgin Mary to love is therefore less happy than we are.

One day she said, regarding having entrusted some intentions to Our Lady, "The Blessed Virgin really carried out my messages well; I'll give her some once more!"[33] And another time she said, "When I think of how much trouble I've had all my life trying to recite the Rosary!"[34] She asked Céline, her infirmarian, to pray much for her to Our Lady.

Thérèse, who tried to offer everything she did in a spiritual way told Pauline, "Sometimes I wanted to have a real dinner and I took a grape, then a mouthful of wine (She could consume very little nourishment during her last illness) and these I offered to the Blessed Virgin. Then I did the same thing for the Child Jesus and my little dinner was finished."[35]

Pauline recalls, "she was showing me the picture of Our Lady of Victories, to which she had pasted the little flower Papa had given her on the day she had confided her vocation to him; the root was detached from it and the

Infant Jesus seemed to be holding it, while He and the Blessed Virgin smiled at her: [the Saint said] 'The little flower has lost its root; this will tell you I'm on my way to Heaven.'[36] Pauline tells us 'after gazing a long time on the statue of the Blessed Virgin [Thérèse said] 'who could ever invent the Blessed Virgin?''[37] Also from Pauline we learn of the following. One day, "when the Angelus was ringing [the Saint asked]: 'Must I extend my little hands?' I answered: 'No, you're even too weak to recite the Angelus. Call upon the Blessed Virgin by simply saying: 'Virgin Mary!' She said: 'Virgin Mary, I love you with all my heart.'"[38]

"I [Pauline] was telling her she suffered less during the silence [the Saint said,] 'Oh! just the opposite! I suffered very much, very much! But it's to the Blessed Virgin that I complained.'"[39]

Thérèse prayed, "O good Blessed Virgin, come to my aid!"[40] In her time of her sickness and great suffering the Saint turned to her Mother.

During her last agony she prayed to Our Lady and at six o'clock in the evening when she heard the bell for the Angelus looked toward the statue of the Virgin of the Smile. Some time before, in one of her poems, she had made the request that Our Blessed Mother would be with her at the eventide after her life and would once again smile at her.

It is therefore quite correct to say that her prayer was Marian, dedicated to the Mother of Jesus at Nazareth and Our Lady of Sorrows at Calvary. She also had a special devotion to The Virgin of the Smile. All through her life she remained a Child of Mary and prayed to Our Lady with childlike faith and confidence. The last words she ever wrote explained, in words written to Our Blessed Mother, that if she, Thérèse, were the Queen of Heaven and Our Lady was little Thérèse - she would want Mary to be the Queen of Heaven.

To the Child Jesus

Thérèse is perhaps, most well known for her love and devotion to the Child or Infant Jesus. She valued the richness of this devotion. She often prayed to the Infant Jesus as she placed flowers before His statue in the Carmel, a duty she was very pleased to fulfill. In this devotion she was completely faithful to the Carmelite tradition. After all, could not the Child Jesus see the mountain of Carmel from Nazareth? Perhaps the Holy Family had even visited this holy place of the prophet Elijah.

In the reform of Carmel, St Teresa of Avila promoted devotion to the Infant Jesus. Once, as she was going through the convent she saw a little child. Before she could speak, the child asked, "Who are you?" The Saint replied "Teresa of Jesus." The child said, "I'm Jesus of Teresa."

The Carmelites carried on this devotion of St Teresa to the Infant Jesus. Father Nemec, tells us in his book, "*The Great and Little One of Prague*", that another Carmelite, "the Venerable Father Francis of Jesus had promoted the age-old tradition of love for the Divine Infant in their Carmels."[41] The beloved statue of the Infant of Prague was originally from Spain. In Spain there was a special devotion to the Holy Infant thanks to St Teresa of Avila. The statue was brought to Prague and was placed in the Chapel of the Carmelites there. It was to a Carmelite, Father Cyril of the Mother of God that the Infant Jesus spoke, saying, "The more you honour me, the more I will bless you." It was to the Belgian Carmelite, The venerable Margaret of the Blessed Sacrament that there were revelations about the foundation of a confraternity, "The Family of the Infant Jesus."

Thérèse, even before she was a Carmelite, had great devotion to the Infant Jesus. She hoped that, as a Carmelite, she would have the name she did later receive - Sister Thérèse of the Child Jesus. "Well, that morning [before visiting the Carmelite nuns] I was wondering what my name would be in religion; Carmel had its Teresa of Jesus already and yet it wouldn't do to give up the name Thérèse, such a lovely name. And all at once I remembered my devotion to the Sacred Infancy and thought how wonderful it would be to be called Thérèse of The Child Jesus. I didn't say anything about this daydream of mine; sure enough, when dear Mother Marie Gonzague asked the sisters what I ought to be called, this dream - name of mine was the one they thought of. How pleased I was! It looked like a special favour from the Child Jesus, this happy piece of thought-transference."[42]

Today too few value this excellent devotion - to the Child Jesus. Perhaps they do not understand. Or perhaps they consider themselves too intellectual for this devotion. A strange intellectualism that would be since among the most faithful to devotion to the Child Jesus we find the writer and intellectual Paul Claudel, who wrote an inspiring poem about this devotion and the brilliant philosopher Saint Edith Stein who carried a picture of the Infant Jesus to her death. No, this devotion is not childish. Yet perhaps to appreciate it one must become childlike. "Unless you become as a little child."

In the letters of Thérèse we find references to her beloved friend the Child Jesus. To Pauline she writes, just before her First Holy Communion, thanking her for a prayer book. "What lovely prayers at the beginning! I said them to the little Child Jesus with all my heart."[43] As a nun the Saint wrote a note to her sister Marie which had a special request. "l should like the candles of the Child Jesus to be lit when I go to Chapter [for her profession.][44]

To one of the nuns, Sister Marie of the Trinity, Thérèse wrote, "May the Divine Child Jesus find in your soul a dwelling all fragrant with the roses of love; may

He find the burning lamp of fraternal charity to warm His frozen limbs and rejoice His small Heart, making Him forget the ingratitude of souls which do not love Him enough."[45]

To the Holy Face of Jesus

Thérèse was greatly devoted to the Holy Face of Jesus. She said that this was the essence of all her spirituality. First, let us outline the history of this devotion. Devotion to the face of Jesus began with St Veronica. Bravely she made her way to Jesus to wipe His face. Some doubt the history of this event. What we should remember is that it was a very common custom in those days to offer the veil that was worn around the neck to tired travelers and friends as they arrived at one's house. We know that the women showed great courage during the Crucifixion. Surely one of them could have thought of this custom and have been fearless enough to go through the crowds and wipe the face of Jesus. That Our Blessed Lord would reward with a miracle this act of kindness and bravery is just like Him.

The devotion to the Holy Face of Jesus was, originally, a devotion to an image depicting the face of Jesus on the Veil of St Veronica. In the East devotion was to the miraculous icon entitled, "Not Painted By Human Hands." This icon is of the Holy Face of Jesus on the Veil of St Veronica. When the Holy Shroud of Turin was photographed the Church received another precious gift. Photographs of the image of the face of Jesus increased this devotion. The essence of devotion to the Holy Face is the suffering Jesus endured during the Passion and that the marks of suffering seem to hide, yet cannot hide, the Divine look of the face of Jesus. In this century, the Italian mystic Sister Pierina de Micheli, "insists upon the importance of giving this devotion a reparatory aspect."[46] Meaning our love and prayers should be offered to Jesus in reparation for all He suffered, for the wounds and bruises He endured on His face.

Among the saints devoted to the Holy Face of Our Blessed Lord we find the Benedictine nun of Helfta, Germany, St Gertrude the Great (d. 1301) who wrote a beautiful prayer in honour of the Holy Face of Jesus and who received revelations about this devotion. Another apostle of devotion to the Face of Jesus was St Mechtilde (d. 1298) a fellow nun and companion of St Gertrude. The great Franciscan mystic and "Teacher of Theology," Blessed Angela of Foligno (d. 1309) was especially devoted to the Holy Face. St Bonaventure (d.1274) the great "Seraphic Doctor," wrote about the Holy Face of Jesus. He wrote of the sufferings of Our Blessed Lord. He wrote, "Behold the Adorable Face of your Beloved Saviour, Jesus Christ, O Christian soul and lift not your eyes without compassion and behold how much affliction He endures, to seek you, to find you. Open wide your eyes to behold the Holy Face of Jesus Christ. Hear Him attentively! If ever, in inexpressible suffering, He utters a word, hide it when you have heard it as the most precious treasure in the coffer of your heart."[47]

Devotion to the Holy Face increased in France due to the efforts of the Carmelite mystic, Sister Marie of St Pierre (d.1848) of the Carmel of Tours. Sister had received revelations regarding making reparation to the Holy Face. It was in Tours that we find the saintly Leon Dupont (d.1876) called the "Holy Man of Tours." His home, which had a beautiful oratory to the Holy Face of Jesus, was only a few streets from the Carmel of Sister Marie of St Pierre. Mr Dupont built the oratory at the encouragement of Sister Marie. It was ultimately from Tours that Thérèse would learn about devotion to the Holy Face of Jesus.

How Thérèse learned this devotion is interesting. She learned this special devotion from her sister Pauline. Her "Little Mother," had heard about this devotion from Mother Genevieve the foundress of their Carmel. Mother Genevieve had learned of this great devotion from the Carmel of Tours. After hearing of the revelations to Sister Marie Mother Genevieve sent to the Carmel of Tours for mementos of Sister Marie and for novenas to the Holy Face of Our Lord.

So the devotion of Thérèse to the Holy Face of Jesus, which through her was promoted throughout the Church, was learned from her "sister" in Carmel, Sister Marie of St Pierre. It is as if God chose one Carmelite to carry on the work of another. A third Carmelite, Thérèse's sister Céline, also had a mission to fulfill, for it was Céline who painted the picture of the Holy Face of Jesus from the image on the Holy Shroud of Turin. This painting, copied and printed on holy cards, was granted indulgences by Pope Pius XI. It is venerated by Catholics throughout the world. After she was in Carmel, for some time, Thérèse received permission to add to her name "and of the Holy Face." She was then Sister Thérèse of the Child Jesus and of the Holy Face. This devotion was not only part of the spirituality of the Saint, it was also a great consolation during her father's illness. She saw the "suffering servant" in her father who had offered himself as a victim. During his illness his face became distorted.

In reference to the devotion to the Holy Face of Jesus, Thérèse wrote to Céline of the hidden beauty of Jesus. More and more towards the end of the Saint's life her devotion to the Holy Face became the essence of her spirituality.

Thérèse saw behind the downcast eyes of Jesus the beauty of His soul; His bloodstained face revealed His love. She encouraged Céline to contemplate His eyes which have lost their "light" and are downcast, to contemplate His wounds, to look at the Face of Jesus!

There, she told her sister, she would recognize how much He loves us.

She not only contemplated the Holy Face. She wished to be like Our Lord. Our Lord's Divinity was, as it were, hidden during the Passion. She encouraged Céline to be another Veronica and wipe away the blood and tears of Jesus. She kept a picture of the Holy Face of Jesus at her place in the choir and asked that one be placed on one of the curtains of her bed during her last illness. As an outpouring of her love she composed a Consecration to the Holy Face of Jesus. Towards the end of her life she wrote a hymn in honour of the Holy Face. For her day of special honour to the Holy Face of Our Lord she chose the Feast of the Transfiguration.

To St Joseph and the Saints

Like a true child of St Teresa of Avila, the "Little Flower" had a great devotion to, and trust in, St Joseph. The great reformer of Carmel, St Teresa of Avila, had a very great devotion to St Joseph. Father Henri Rondet, S. J. writes, "Among the Carmelites who were devoted to St Joseph, one name dominates all the rest, that of St Teresa of Avila."[48] When she was twenty-six St Teresa was cured of a very serious illness through the intercession of St Joseph. She then became a very enthusiastic apostle of devotion to him, seeing to it that his feast was kept with great solemnity. She stated that those who pray to him would receive the gift of prayer. St Teresa of Avila was very glad to dedicate the first reformed Carmel to St Joseph, as she had been instructed to do by Our Lord. Also, two-thirds of the other foundations she made were dedicated to St Joseph! In her "Life" she wrote beautifully about this Saint. She said, "I wish I could persuade everybody to be devoted to this glorious Saint, for much experience has taught me what blessings he can obtain from God for us. Of all those I have known with a true devotion and particular veneration for St Joseph, not one has failed to advance in virtue. He helps those who turn to him to make real progress. For several years now, I believe, I have always made some request to him on his feast day and it has always been granted; and when my request is not quite what it ought to be, he puts it right for my greater benefit."[49]

Thérèse was a faithful follower of St Teresa of Avila regarding devotion to Saint Joseph. We read in *"The Last Conversations"* about how St Thérèse was casting some flowers at a statue of St Joseph in the garden saying in a child-like tone, 'take them.' Pauline asked her if she were doing this to obtain a special favour? The Saint answered that it wasn't her reason at all. She was doing it just to please him; that she didn't give in order to receive.

Along with St Joseph, Thérèse had special devotion to a to a number of saints. She often prayed to the saints. She, of course, was devoted to St Teresa of Avila, her namesake and to St John of the Cross, her teacher of the spiritual life. She was also especially devoted to the martyrs. Since she was a child when she and Céline would read and talk about the brave martyrs, she had a special love and devotion to them. She had a special friendship with St Cecilia and St Agnes. She tells us in her autobiography - "Until I made this pilgrimage to Rome, I'd never had any special devotion for St Cecilia; but now I had the chance of visiting her house, which has become a church, the actual scene of her martyrdom... So now I felt something more than a special devotion for St Cecilia, a real bond of friendship with her. She became a favourite, a confidante to whom I entrust my secrets."[50]

Pauline tell the following story: "We were showing her a picture of Joan of Arc in her prison [Thérèse said,] 'The saints encourage me, too, in my prison. They tell me: As long as you are in irons, you cannot carry out your mission, but later on, after your death, this will be the time for your works and your conquests."[51]

In Rome, during her pilgrimage, she made her way, with Céline, into the floor of the Coliseum in order to kiss the actual place where the martyrs had died for their faith. She also was very glad to bring home stones from the Church of St Agnes. Thérèse was also very devoted to the St Joan of Arc. She felt that like St Joan she was called to be a saint. She portrayed St Joan in a play that she composed for her fellow Carmelites. Also, during the last years of her life, she had a very special devotion to Theophane Venard, a priest of the Paris Foreign Mission Society, who was martyred in Hanoi. She read his biography and letters and often wrote about him in her letters to her missionary brothers. During her last illness she kept a picture of him near her. She spoke about him often during her last illness. When one of her sisters was arranging the room and not being careful of the picture of Theophane, she told her to be careful of his picture. When she told Pauline that she would be the last of the sisters to die she promised that she and Theophane would come find her. Often during her last illness she prayed to this missionary and kissed the picture. She considered him a great saint. Theophane Venard was later beatified by Pope Saint Pius X in 1909.

The essence of Thérèse's devotion to the saints is love. Her devotion is affection. The saints are simply part of her family and she loves them dearly and talks to them familiarly and when they do not answer her prayers she "loves them all the more!"

Thérèse had a great desire to be a saint so it was normal that she had this "family relation" to the saints in Heaven. She considered herself their little sister and she prayed to them with great confidence. She was especially inspired by a dream she had of the Venerable Anne of Jesus in which this Carmelite, who had brought the

Carmelite Nuns of the Reform to France, covered her with her mantle and answered her question telling her that God was pleased with her little offerings, her way of spirituality.

What is most inspiring about Thérèse's devotion to the saints is her trust, confidence and childlike friendship. She perfectly combined respect and friendliness. On the Feast of St Joachim she said it was grandpapa's feast day!

Love for the Blessed Sacrament

Thérèse was a true Carmelite in that she had a very ardent love for the Blessed Sacrament. St Teresa of Avila is well known for her vigils by the tabernacle. St John of the Cross was very devoted to the Blessed Sacrament.

In France Carmel received many graces from this country's piety, such as devotion to the Sacred Heart and adoration of the Blessed Sacrament exposed. France is the country of St Margaret Mary and Mother Mary of Jesus and Mother Mary of St Peter, foundresses of communities of nuns of perpetual adoration. In France we find Montmarte, the national shrine to the Sacred Heart and Eucharistic confraternities such as the "Guard of Honour." The French Carmelite Father Augustine of the Blessed Sacrament was greatly devoted to the Holy Eucharist. Better known as Herman Cohen, this great pianist was instantly converted from Judaism one day when he simply looked at the Blessed Sacrament in the monstrance.

France is the country where began the devotion of offering reparation to the Blessed Sacrament - for irreverence or lack of love and appreciation.

Thérèse was very devoted to the Blessed Sacrament all throughout her life. As a child she enjoyed making daily visits to the Blessed Sacrament with her father. During her retreat at the Abbey before her First Holy Communion the following happened.

"One morning, I remember, I was sent to the infirmary because I had a bad cough. (Ever since my illness, the nuns had taken great care of me; whenever I had a slight headache, or looked paler than usual, I was either sent outside to get some fresh air or to rest in the infirmary.) And then dear Céline came in; she had got leave to come and see me, though I was in retreat, so as to present me with a picture which delighted me highly - what do you think it was? The little flower at the door of the tabernacle."[52]

Remembering her First Holy Communion the Saint wrote, "What comfort it brought to me, that first kiss Our Lord imprinted on my soul! A lover's kiss; I knew that I was loved, and I, in my turn, told Him that I loved Him and was giving myself to Him for all eternity. It was a long time now since He had made any demands on me; there had been no struggles, no sacrifices; we had exchanged looks, He and I, insignificant though I was and we had understood one another. And now it wasn't a question of looks, something had melted away and there were no longer two of us - Thérèse had simply disappeared, like a drop lost in the ocean; Jesus only was left, my Master, my King. Hadn't I begged him to take away my liberty, because I was so afraid of the use I made of it, Hadn't I longed, weak and helpless as I was, to be united once for all, with that divine strength?

"So deep was my joy, so overpowering, that I couldn't contain myself; before long, tears of happiness were pouring down my cheeks to the astonishment of my companions. They didn't realize what happens when all the joys of Heaven come flooding into a human heart, how difficult it was for that heart, still in exile, to stand the strain of the impact without finding relief in tears... I had no room for any feeling but joy and felt closer to her than ever, wasn't she just giving herself up irrevocably, to Him who came so lovingly and gave Himself to me?"

"The day after my first Communion was still one of happiness but overcast with melancholy...I couldn't be content with anything less than our Lord's presence. How I longed for the day when I should be able to receive Him again! About a month later, when I went to get shriven [forgiven, when she went to confession] for Ascensiontide, I took my courage in both hands and asked if I might go to Communion. To my surprise, the priest consented and I found myself kneeling at the Holy Table between Papa and Marie. This second Communion, too, has left touching memories behind it; I was shedding tears still, but with an indescribable sense of consolation and I kept on repeating to myself these words of St Paul: 'I am alive; rather, not I; it is Christ that lives in me!' From then on, my longing for our Lord's presence continued to increase and I got permission to communicate on all great feasts."[53]

The First Holy Communion of Thérèse was extremely fervent. And on that day she remembered to pray for a special intention. She tells us in her autobiography. "When I went for walks with Papa, he was fond of sending me to give money to the poor people we met. One day, we saw a man dragging himself painfully along on crutches, but when I went up to him with my penny he turned out not to be as poor as all that, he smiled sadly and wouldn't take it. I can't describe my emotions; here was this man I should have liked to comfort and console and instead of that I'd injured his feelings. I dare say the poor cripple guessed what was passing through my mind, because he turned back to smile at me. How would it be to give him the cake Papa had just bought for me? No, I hadn't the courage but I did wish I could offer him something, something it would be impossible to refuse; I felt so sorry for him. Then I remembered having been told that on your First Communion day you could get any prayer granted. That was a comforting thought; I was only six years old then, but when I made my First

Communion I promised I would remember my poor man. That promise I kept, five years later and I hope the prayer was answered; a prayer God Himself had inspired; a prayer for one of his suffering members."[54]

In Carmel Thérèse suffered from the fact that the nuns could receive Holy Communion so seldom. "After all Our Lord doesn't come down from Heaven every day just to wait there in a gold ciborium."[55] During her last illness this privation was extremely painful for her. Her last Holy Communion was on 19th August; she died on 30th September.

Once when Thérèse was cleaning the chapel a novice saw her kneeling before the altar reach up and tap on the tabernacle door. She heard Thérèse say, "Art thou there Jesus? I beseech Thee to speak to me." She stayed for a few seconds with her head gently resting against the tabernacle and then she turned around. The novice said that the Saint's face was absolutely transfigured and completely shining with joy.

It is quite well known how much Thérèse was devoted to her favourite occupation in Carmel, that of being sacristan. She loved to look in the chalice and at the paten, seeing her reflection, realizing that soon the Holy Eucharist would be there. She would also kiss the large priest's alter bread that would be consecrated and also the corporal.

Few have written about her great reverence for the Blessed Sacrament. We are fortunate that John Beevers, writing about this in "*The Storm of Glory*", included the following significant incidents. "One day after Mass St Thérèse discovered a Particle of the Sacred Host on the corporal. She ran to the laundry where her novices were and signaled for them to follow her. Back in the sacristy they knelt in adoration. There was a similar incident: a novice met St Thérèse in the cloister. St Thérèse said, in a low, intense voice; 'follow me. I am carrying Jesus.' She was coming from the altar where she had found a Fragment of the Sacred Host and she was carrying It to the sacristy, after sending a message to the priest. The two nuns knelt in adoration before Our Blessed Lord until the priest arrived."[56]

Today, when, unfortunately, so few are concerned about Particles of the Blessed Sacrament, Thérèse could be a good teacher of sound theology and devout reverence. Many people seem to have forgotten that the Particles from a Consecrated Host are Our Saviour Jesus Christ. To be concerned about Them is not a scruple but rather sound theology and devout reverence and faithful imitation of Thérèse of Lisieux.

St Thérèse, apostle of prayer

To be a Carmelite means to be an apostle of prayer. It is a life dedicated to prayer and penance for the salvation of souls and for priests. St Teresa of Avila had these intentions in mind when she founded the reform Carmels. She wanted her nuns to be apostles of prayer for the salvation of souls. St Teresa, living during the Counter Reformation was truly very much concerned about the work of priests, bishops, preachers and theologians. Their work was very important and St Teresa encouraged her nuns to pray and offer penance for their work and thereby aid, and share in, their apostolate.

In *"The Way of Perfection"* St Teresa of Avila tells her nuns, "If your prayers and desires and disciplines and fasts are not performed for the intentions of which I have spoken, reflect and believe that you are not carrying out the work of fulfilling the object for which the Lord has brought you here."[57]

The Carmelite nuns to this day are very faithful to their apostolate of prayer, especially for priests. Mother Catherine Thomas of Divine Providence, O.C.D. in her book *"My Beloved"* expresses this in words reminiscent of St Teresa of Avila when she writes, "Carmel, from the very first week of postulancy, impressed me as being a spiritual headquarters far up in the battle area. The nuns seemed almost to stand at attention whenever the Prioress read an urgent request for prayers. Prayer seemed like a sort of warfare; silence was our fortress; penance and mortification were our strategy."[58]

Many things to pray for

Thérèse was faithful to this Carmelite tradition and prayed much for the salvation of souls, for priests and for the missions. When she prayed for her missionary "brothers" it was to help them to work for the salvation of souls. She even promised that from Heaven she would stop babies from dying until they were baptized. She not only prayed for the salvation of souls, she suffered for them and even offered her life as a victim on their behalf. The salvation of souls by prayer and suffering was the apostolate of Thérèse. She refers to this apostolate in her letters to Céline who was called to this vocation, also. She urged her sister to spend her time well and help to save souls.

She realized correctly that reparation for sin and the salvation of souls are closely related. She wanted to save souls so that these souls would love God for all eternity. She knew that this was her vocation and that this was in keeping with the Carmelite tradition. This was her apostolate of prayer - dedicated to salvation and reparation. Like St

Teresa of Avila, she would be an apostle, a missionary with her two "weapons" of prayer and penance.

Thérèse, in her autobiography, explained the effectiveness of prayer in an interesting way. "'Give me a lever and a fulcrum.' said the man of science, 'and I'll shift the world.' Archimedes wasn't talking to God, so his request wasn't granted and in any case he was only thinking of the material world. But the saints really have enjoyed the privilege he asked for; the fulcrum God told them to use was Himself, nothing less than Himself and the lever was prayer. Only it must be the kind of prayer that sets the heart all on fire with love; that's how the saints shift the world in our own day and that's how they'll do it to the end of time."[59]

To her sister Céline she wrote that the two of them should pray for priests, that their lives should be consecrated to praying for them. She believed, she told her sister, every day Jesus made her feel that this was His will for them.

But she did not only pray for important intentions. She prayed for little things, too. Every need, she believed, called for prayer. In writing to her cousin Jeanne, she wrote, "I am also asking that his pharmacy may find a buyer."[60] She wrote to her aunt telling her that she had said many prayers that her aunt's nasty sprain may disappear completely. And to her cousin the Saint wrote that she prayed for my dearest uncle and my dearest aunt more and more.

To the Abbé Belliere (her missionary "brother") Thérèse wrote that she was happy to write to him but felt prayer and suffering were the surest way to save souls.

To Père Rouland (the other missionary "brother") she wrote, "I say many prayers for yours [his parents still on earth; I find it a most sweet obligation and I promise you always to fulfill it faithfully, even if I leave this external veil more so perhaps, for I should better know the graces they need; and then, when their course here below is finished, I shall come and seek them out in your name and introduce them to Heaven"[61]

When she was dying the Saint wrote the following to Abbé Belliere, "Ah! I beg you pray hard for me, prayers are so necessary for me at this moment, but especially pray for our Mother."[62] Here "Mother" means Pauline, her "little mother."

Praying to Thérèse

Many people throughout the world have prayed and do pray to St Thérèse. And their prayers have been and are heard. To begin considering praying to this great Saint I'll quote several paragraphs from John Beevers' book "*The Storm of Glory*". In this interesting book we read, "Earlier in this chapter, mention was made of Thérèse touching her crucifix with rose petals and then urging her sisters to keep them. In May 1910 a man named Ferdinand Aubry, aged sixty, entered the home for the aged kept by the Little Sisters of the Poor at Lisieux. He was very weak, following an attack of paralysis. In August ulcers developed on his tongue, gangrene set in and towards the end of September the tongue began to split up. The doctor could do nothing. The Mother Superior of the home read to Aubry the story Thérèse tells of the old man she tried to help with money when she was a little girl and he at once grew confident that she would help him. But he grew worse and more fragments of his tongue fell away. On the 28th the Little Sisters sent to the Carmel and asked for one of the rose petals Thérèse had been so certain would be of use after her death. It came in a little sachet. Ferdinand tore it open and with great difficulty swallowed the petal. He immediately felt better and on 2nd October said to the sister nursing him: 'I am cured.' He was. So much of his tongue had been destroyed that his words could hardly be understood but he asked the doctor if, now that the disease had gone, his tongue would grow whole. He was of course, told that this was impossible but, undaunted, he continued his prayers to Thérèse. Three weeks later his tongue was whole again! This was attested by the sisters and by the doctor who attached a photograph of the restored tongue to his attestation.

"In Glasgow, Mrs Dorans suffered from an abdominal tumor. Towards the end of April, 1909 she was examined

by several doctors. They all agreed that an operation would
be useless as the tumor was too deeply rooted. She grew
steadily weaker and for ten weeks could take no solid food
…her condition worsened and on 22nd August, 1909, her
Protestant doctor said she had not much longer to live. On
that day a friend came to see her and suggested making a
novena to Thérèse. It was begun that day, a Sunday. During
the four following days Mrs Dorans sank rapidly and on
Thursday she was not expected to live till the following
morning. At eleven o'clock at night she was given a little
ice to suck. It brought on a violent attack of vomiting. Then
she fell asleep until about half-past five in the morning.
She was awakened by what she described as a light touch
on her shoulder, although she was alone in the room except
for one of her daughters who, exhausted by the strain of
nursing, had fallen fast asleep. Mrs Dorans felt no pain.
She put her hand on the site of the tumor and, with
astonished joy, discovered the growth had gone. Calling
her daughter, she asked for something to drink and
swallowed a large glass of soda water. A little later, she
wanted tea and something to eat. Her daughter, thinking
she was humoring the whim of a dying woman, prepared
and gave her tea and a roll. Mrs Dorans drank the tea and
ate half the roll. When the doctor came, he expected to find
her dead; instead, she was sitting up in great good spirits.
Bewildered, he spent an hour examining her and found
every organ in her body working properly and the tumor

gone, leaving behind a small lump the size of a marble. He gave a certificate stating that she was cured. From that time Mrs Dorans lived a completely normal life.

"Less than six years after Thérèse's death, one Madame Jouanne, the wife of a gardener at Marnes-la-Coquette was operated upon for a double strangulated hernia. She nearly died and remained an invalid after her recovery from the operation. A year later she had appendicitis, complicated by general peritonitis. The two miracles selected for the beatification of Thérèse were the healing of a native of Lisieux, a twenty-three-year-old man named Charles Anne who was studying for the priesthood, and the cure of Sister Louise of St Germain, one of the Daughters of the Cross at Ustarritz in the south of France.

"Normally, three miracles are required to be proved, but two only are needed where many witnesses have known the servant of God.

"Charles Anne was attacked by tuberculosis as he was studying for the priesthood at the diocesan seminary in Bayeux. By September 1906 he was dying with grave lesions in both lungs. He wore round his neck a sachet containing a wisp of Thérèse's hair and after a terrifying hemorrhage he cried out to her: 'I did not come to the seminary to die. I came to work for God. You must cure me!' Clutching the relic he fell asleep. When he awoke he was cured. His doctor reported that his lungs were completely restored and added: 'This cure is absolutely extraordinary and inexplicable from a scientific point of view.' The young man became a priest and was in Rome for the ceremony of the beatification of Thérèse on 29th April 1923.

"Sister Louise fell ill of an ulcer in the stomach early in 1913. Medical treatment had no effect and in 1915 she was thought to be dying and received the last sacraments. She did not die but the ulcer remained. The next year she began a novena - the second to Thérèse. During the night of 10th September she had a vision of Thérèse who said to her: 'Be generous with God I promise you, you will soon be cured.' When she woke in the morning the floor around her bed was strewn with rose petals and no one was able to explain how they got there. She grew worse but slept peacefully throughout the night of 25th September. Next morning she was well and at once joined in the ordinary activities of her community. Her doctor's certification of the cure was confirmed by X-rays.

"These two cases were thoroughly examined by the Sacred Congregation of Rites in Rome and six medical specialists, three for each cure, separately gave a written review of the case and their conclusion. All agreed that the cures were miraculous.

"Two more miracles were required to be proved before Thérèse was canonized. An account of them is given by Pius Xl in the Papal Bull canonizing Thérèse. The Pope's words are: "The two miracles proposed for discussion were these: first, the cure of Gabriella Trimusi; the other, the cure of Marie Pellmans. Gabriella, who entered the Congregation of the Poor Sisters of the Sacred Heart at the age of twenty-three (whose Mother House is situated at Parma) in the year 1913, began to suffer in her left knee; she was in the habit of breaking firewood across her knee and this caused a lesion at the joint which prepared the way for a tuberculosis infection. The trouble began with a dull pain, then the knee became swollen and finally loss of appetite brought about emaciation.

"She was attended by two physician but without result, so that, three years later she was sent to Milan, where injections, sun-baths and various other remedies were tried in vain; after four years the spinal column became affected. Then the sister returned to Parma, where she was visited by several doctors who diagnosed the disease as being a case of tubercular lesion and prescribed general remedies.

"The ordinary physician to the Parma community, noting the growing gravity of the case especially with regard to the spine, advised sending her to a public hospital. A radiograph of the knee was taken before her removal which showed the existence of periostitis at the head of the tibia. On being taken to hospital she was once more subjected to X-rays and whilst there was attacked by Spanish influenza, which caused fresh and constantly increasing pain in the vertebral column. When all remedies had failed she was advised by a priest on 13th June, 1923 to join in a public novena in honour of Blessed Thérèse of the Child Jesus. She took part in the prayers, more concerned for the health of the other sisters than her own. The close of the novena coincided with the close of a tridium in a neighboring Carmelite church and several of the nuns, including the sick sister, sought permission to attend the ceremony. Sister Trimusi, on her return, after slowly and painfully effecting the short journey, entered the chapel of the community where the sisters were already assembled. The Superioress exhorted Sister Gabriella to pray with confidence and go to her place. Strange to say, the invalid knelt unthinkingly on her knee without feeling the slightest pain, although she did not realize what she had done owing to the greatly increased pain from which she was suffering at that moment in her spine. She went to supper with the sisters and after the meal was finished, slowly mounted the stairs and, going into the first room she came across, took off the apparatus which she wore to support the spine, exclaiming in a loud voice: 'I am cured! I am cured!'

"She at once returned to the labors and exercises of religious life which she began to fulfil without either pain or fatigue, giving thanks to God on account of the miracle wrought through the intercession of Blessed Thérèse of the Child Jesus.

"The skilled doctors appointed by the Sacred Congregation of Rites discussed the miracle at great length and decided that the lesion at the knee was chronic arthrosynovitis and that the spinal trouble was chronic spondilitis. These two organic lesions, which had resisted all treatment, yielded to Divine Omnipotence and Sister Gabriella, by a miracle, recovered her health completely.

"The story of the second miracle, that of Marie Pellmans, can be related more briefly.

"In the month of October 1919 she fell a victim of pulmonary tuberculosis, followed by gastritis and enteritis, both likewise of a tubercular nature. She was medically attended first at home and afterwards in a sanatorium named La Hulpe. She returned home in August... In the month of March 1923, she went in company with some other pilgrims to the Carmel of Lisieux and while praying before the tomb of Blessed Thérèse, and confidently invoking her aid, she was perfectly cured."

"These miracles were of course done, not by the power of Thérèse, but by the power of God through her intercession. St Thomas Aquinas puts the matter briefly: "The working of miracles is directed to the confirmation of faith... it proceeds from God's omnipotence on which faith relies.. true miracles cannot be wrought save by the power of God, because God works them for man's benefit, and this in two ways: in one way for the confirmation of truth declared, in another way in proof of a person's holiness, which God desires to propose as an example of virtue."[63]

Praying with St Thérèse

Litany to St Thérèse

Lord, have mercy on us.
Christ, have mercy on us.
Lord, have mercy on us.
Christ, hear us.
Christ, graciously hear us.
God the Father of Heaven,
have mercy on us.
God the Son, Redeemer of the world, *have mercy on us.*
God the Holy Spirit, *have mercy on us.*
Holy Trinity, One God, *have mercy on us.*

Holy Mary, Mother of God, *pray for us.*
Our Lady of Victory, *pray for us.*
Our Lady of Mount Carmel, *...etc.*
Saint Thérèse of the Child Jesus,
Saint Thérèse of the Holy Face,
Saint Thérèse, spouse of Jesus,
Saint Thérèse, child of Mary,
Saint Thérèse, devoted to Saint Joseph,
Saint Thérèse, angel of innocence,

Saint Thérèse, model child,
Saint Thérèse, pattern of religious,
Saint Thérèse, flower of Carmel,
Saint Thérèse, zealous to save souls,
Saint Thérèse, converter of hardened hearts,
Saint Thérèse, healer of the diseased,
Saint Thérèse, filled with love for the Blessed Sacrament,
Saint Thérèse, filled with angelic fervour,
Saint Thérèse, filled with loyalty to the Holy Father,
Saint Thérèse, filled with a tender love for the Church,
Saint Thérèse, filled with extraordinary
    love for God and neighbour,
Saint Thérèse, wounded with a heavenly flame,
Saint Thérèse, victim of divine love,
Saint Thérèse, patient in sufferings,
Saint Thérèse, eager for humiliations,
Saint Thérèse, consumed with love of God,
Saint Thérèse, rapt in ecstasy,
Saint Thérèse, dedicated to pray for priests,
Saint Thérèse, who refused God nothing,
Saint Thérèse, who desired always to be as a little child,
Saint Thérèse, who taught the way of spiritual childhood,
Saint Thérèse, who gave perfect example of trust in God,
Saint Thérèse, whom Jesus filled
    with a desire for suffering,
Saint Thérèse, who found perfection in little things,
Saint Thérèse, who sought bitterness in this life,

Saint Thérèse, who told us to call thee "little Thérèse,"
Saint Thérèse, who gained countless souls for Christ,
Saint Thérèse, who promised after thy death
   a shower of roses,
Saint Thérèse, who foretold:
   "I will spend my Heaven doing good upon earth,"
Saint Thérèse, Patroness of the Missions,

Lamb of God, who takes away the sins of the world,
spare us, O Lord.
Lamb of God, who takes away the sins of the world,
graciously hear us, O Lord.
Lamb of God, who takes away the sins of the world,
have mercy on us.

V. Pray for us, Saint Thérèse,
R. That we may be made worthy
   of the promises of Christ.

Let us pray

Hear our prayer, O Lord, we beseech thee, as we venerate
Saint Thérèse, thy virgin and martyr of love longing to
make thee loved, and grant us, through her intercession,
the gift of childlike simplicity and the spirit of complete
dedication to thy divine service. Amen.[64]

Litany to Saint Thérèse

Lord, have mercy on us.
Christ, have mercy on us.
Lord, have mercy on us.
Christ, hear us.
Christ, graciously hear us.
God the Father of Heaven, *have mercy on us*.
God the Son, Redeemer of the world, *have mercy on us*.
God the Holy Spirit, *have mercy on us*.
Holy Trinity, One God, *have mercy on us*.

Holy Mary, *pray for us*,
Our Lady of Victory, *pray for us*,
Saint Thérèse, servant of God, *...etc*.
Saint Thérèse, victim of the merciful love of God,
Saint Thérèse, spouse of Jesus,
Saint Thérèse, gift of Heaven
Saint Thérèse, remarkable in childhood,
Saint Thérèse, an example of obedience,
Saint Thérèse, lover of the will of God,
Saint Thérèse, lover of peace,
Saint Thérèse, lover of patience,
Saint Thérèse, lover of gentleness,
Saint Thérèse, heroic in sacrifice,
Saint Thérèse, generous in forgiving,
Saint Thérèse, benefactress of the needy,

Saint Thérèse, lover of Jesus,
Saint Thérèse, devoted to the Holy Face,
Saint Thérèse, consumed with divine love of God,
Saint Thérèse, advocate of extreme cases.
Saint Thérèse, persevering in prayer,
Saint Thérèse, a powerful advocate with God,
Saint Thérèse, showering roses,
Saint Thérèse, doing good upon earth,
Saint Thérèse, answering all prayers,
Saint Thérèse, lover of holy chastity,
Saint Thérèse, lover of voluntary poverty,
Saint Thérèse, lover of obedience,
Saint Thérèse, burning with zeal for God's glory,
Saint Thérèse, inflamed with the Spirit of Love,
Saint Thérèse, child of benediction,
Saint Thérèse, perfect in simplicity,
Saint Thérèse, so remarkable for trust in God
Saint Thérèse, gifted with unusual intelligence,
Saint Thérèse, never invoked without some answer,
Saint Thérèse, teaching us the sure way,
Saint Thérèse, victim of Divine Love,

Lamb of God, who takes away the sins of the world,
spare us, O Lord.
Lamb of God, who takes away the sins of the world,
graciously hear us, O Lord.

Lamb of God, who takes away the sins of the world,
have mercy on us.
Saint Thérèse, the Little Flower of Jesus, *pray for us*.

Let us pray

O God, who inflamed with thy Spirit of Love the soul of
thy servant Thérèse of the Child Jesus, grant that we may
also love thee and may make thee much loved. Amen.[65]

To obtain graces through the intercession
of St Thérèse

O Eternal Father, who art in Heaven, where thou dost
crown the merits of those who in this life serve thee
faithfully, for the sake of the most pure love of thy little
daughter, St Thérèse of the Child Jesus, had for thee, so
as to bind thee to give her whatever she desires, incline
thine ears to the petitions which she offers up to thee on
my behalf, and hear my prayers by granting me the grace
I ask. *Our Father*, *Hail Mary*, *Glory be*.[66]

Prayer to St Thérèse

O little St Thérèse of the Child Jesus, who, during thy
short life on earth became a mirror of angelic purity, of
love strong as death, and of wholehearted abandonment
to God, now that thou rejoicest in the reward of thy
virtues, cast a glance of pity on me as I leave all things in
thy hands. Make my troubles thine own - speak a word

for me to our Lady Immaculate, whose flower of special love thou wert - to that Queen of Heaven "who smiled on thee at the dawn of life." Beg her as the Queen of the Heart of Jesus to obtain for me by her powerful intercession the grace I yearn for so ardently at this moment and that she join with it a blessing that may strengthen me during life. Defend me at the hour of death and lead me straight on to a happy eternity. Amen.[67]

Prayer for missionaries

St Thérèse of the Child Jesus, thou who hast been rightly proclaimed the Patroness of Catholic missions throughout the world, remember the burning desire which thou didst manifest here on earth to plant the Cross of Christ on every shore and to preach the Gospel even to the consummation of the world, we implore thee, according to thy promise, to assist all priests and missionaries and the whole Church of God.[68]

Prayer to the Father

O Father in Heaven, who, through Saint Thérèse of the Child Jesus, dost desire to remind the world of the merciful love that fills thy Heart and the childlike trust we should have in thee, humbly we thank thee for having crowned with so great glory thine ever faithful child and for giving her wondrous power to bring unto thee, day by day, innumerable souls who will praise thee eternally.

Saint Thérèse of the Child Jesus remember thy promise to do good upon earth, shower down thy roses on those who invoke thee and obtain for us from God the graces we hope for from his infinite goodness. O Saint Thérèse of the Child Jesus, who hast merited the title of Patroness of the Catholic Missions throughout the entire world, we beseech thee, according to thy promise, help priests, missionaries, and the whole Church. Amen.[69]

Prayer for spiritual childhood

O my sweet Jesus, give me the charity and simplicity of Saint Thérèse of the Infant Jesus, whose mission in Heaven is to make others love the good God as she loved him, to teach souls her Little Way. Give me such longings that I may not rest until my heart loves God with all my strength, until I arrive at the spiritual childhood of the Little Flower of Jesus. Amen.

Prayer for world peace

O Saint Thérèse, Little Flower of Jesus, who won universal confidence, obtain for all nations the blessing of fraternal union. Exert thy wondrous influence over hearts, so that all the children of the great human family may unite in love of the same Father who is in Heaven. Teach nations and individuals the great law of evangelical charity which thou hast so well understood and practiced here below and dost continue so gloriously now that thou art in Heaven, that a lasting agreement being thus established between nations, the desire of the Vicar of Jesus Christ may be soon realized: the peace as a fruit of Justice and Charity. Amen.

Recommended Reading

Autobiography of a saint: Thérèse of Lisieux, The complete and authorised text of "L'histoire d'une ame", translated by Ronald Knox, foreword by Mgr Vernon Johnson. 1958, Harvill Press Ltd, London.

The Collected Letters of St Thérèse of Lisieux: Translated by F. J. Sheed, preface by Vernon Johnson, 1972, Sheed and Ward Ltd, London.

Spiritual Childhood by Mgr Vernon Johnson, 1953, Sheed and Ward.

Thérèse of Lisieux by Michael Hollings, 1981, Collins, London.

Storm of glory - St.Therese of Lisieux by John Beevers. 1950, Sheed and Ward.

The Spiritual Journey of St Thérèse of Lisieux by Guy Gaucher, 1987 Darton, Longman, and Todd, London.

The Spiritual Genius of St Thérèse of Lisieux by Jean Guitton, 1997, Burns and Oates, UK.

Holy Daring, the Fearless trust of St Thérèse of Lisieux, by John Udris, 1997, Gracewing, UK.

Love in the Heart of the Church: The Mission of St Thérèse of Lisieux, by Christopher O'Donnell O. Carm. Veritas Publications, Dublin 1.

St Thérèse of Lisieux - Poems: Translated by Alan Bancroft, 1996, Fount HarperCollins, London.

Endnotes

1 St Thérèse *Autobiography of St Thérèse of Lisieux*. Translated by Monsignor Ronald Knox (New York, P.J. Kennedy & Sons, 1962).

2 Frances Parkinson Keyes, *Written in Heaven*. (New York, Hawthorne, 1962) Page 174.

3 Conrad De Meester, O.C.D. Editor, *Saint Thérèse of Lisieux Her Life, Times, and Teaching*. (Institute of Carmelite Studies, Washington D.C. 1997) Page 25.

4 *Ibid*. Page 39.

5 *Ibid*. Page 50.

6 *Ibid*. Page 53.

7 St Thérèse, *Autobiography of St Thérèse of Lisieux*, Page 105 & 106.

8 *Ibid*. Page 107.

9 *Ibid*. Page 109.

10 *Ibid*. Page 128.

11 *Ibid*. Pages 128 & 129.

12 *Ibid*. Page 133.

13 John Beevers, *The Storm of Glory*. Page 102.

14 St Thérèse, *Autobiography*, Page 239.

15 John Clarke, O.C.D. St Thérèse, *Her Last Conversations*. (Washington, D.C. Carmelite Studies, 1977) Page 228.

16 *Ibid*. Page 206.

17 St Thérèse, *The Collected Letters*, Page 330.

18 *Ibid*. Page 330.

19 *Ibid*. Page 330 & 331.

20 Rev John Arintero, O.P. *The Mystical Evolution in the Development and Vitality of the Church*, Vol. 11. Translated by Rev Jordan Aumann, O.P. (Rockford, Tan Books, 1978) Page 223.

21 Rev Marie Eugene, O.C.D. *I Am A Daughter of the Church*. Translated by Sister Verda Clare, C.S.C. (Westminster, Christian Classics, 1979) Page 578.

22 Blessed Mary of Jesus Crucified, *Thoughts of Blessed Mary of Jesus Crucified, The Foundress of the Carmel of Bethlehem*. (Bethlehem, Carmel of Bethlehem, 1974) Page 64.

23 Lady Cecil Kerr, *Theresa Helena Higginson*. (Rockford, Tan Books, 1978) Page 229.

24 St John of the Cross, *The Collected Works*. Translated by Rev Kieran Kavanaugh, O.C.D. and Rev Otilio Rodriquez, O.C.D. (Washington, D.C. Carmelite Studies, 1979) Page 592, The Living Flame of Love. No.31 of the First Stanza.

86

[25] St Teresa of Avila, *The Interior Castle*. Translated by E. Allison Peers. (Garden City, Image Books 1961) Page 209.

[26] Rev Francois Jamart, O.C.D. *The Complete Spirituality of St Thérèse*. Page 249.

[27] St Thérèse, *Autobiography*. Pages 106 & 107.

[28] *Ibid*. Page 118.

[29] *Ibid*. Pages 155 & 156.

[30] John Clarke, *Her Last Conversations*. Page 55.

[31] *Ibid*. Page 55.

[32] *Ibid*. Page 60.

[33] *Ibid*. Pages 62 & 63.

[34] Clarke, *Her Last Conversations*. Page 160.

[35] *Ibid*. Pages 139 & 140.

[36] *Ibid*. Page 178.

[37] *Ibid*. Page 177.

[38] *Ibid*. Page 182.

[39] *Ibid*. Page 184.

[40] *Ibid*. Page 204.

[41] Rev Ludvik Nemec, *The Great and Little One of Prague*. (Philadelphia, Reilly, 1959) P. 32.

[42] St Thérèse, *Autobiography*. Page 96.

[43] St Thérèse, *Collected Letters of St Thérèse*. Translated by Frank Sheed (London, Sheed & Ward, 1949) Page 12.

[44] *Ibid*. Page 125.

[45] *Ibid*. Page 304.

[46] Caesar Gill, *In The Splendor of His Countenance*. (Newark, Caesar Gill, 1977) Page 15.

[47] *Ibid*. Pages 14 & 15.

[48] Rev Henri Rondet, S.J. *St Joseph*. Translated by Donald Attwater. (New York, Kennedy, 1956) Page 28.

[49] *Ibid*. Page 76.

[50] St Thérèse, *Autobiography*. Page 166.

[51] Clarke, *Her Last Conversations*, Page 144.

[52] St Thérèse, *Autobiography*. Page 103.

[53] *Ibid*. Pages 107 & 108.

[54] *Ibid*. Page 61.

[55] *Ibid*. Page 135.

[56] John Beevers, *The Storm of Glory*". Pages 107 & 108.

[57] St Teresa of Avila, *The Way of Perfection*. Page 51.

[58] Mother Catherine Thomas of Divine Providence, *My Beloved. The Story of a Carmelite Nun*. Page 260.

[59] St Thérèse, *Autobiography*. Page 311.

[60] St Thérèse, *Collected Letters of St Thérèse*. Page 145.

[61] *Ibid*. Page 293.

[62] *Ibid*. Page 310.

[63] John Beevers, *The Storm of Glory*. Page 123, 124, 126, 127 & 129.

[64] Father Albert J. Herbert, S.M. *Prayerbook of Favourite Litanies.* (Rockford, TAN Books, 1985) Pages 280, 281 & 282.

[65] *Ibid.* Pages 283 & 284.

[66] Sister Gesualda of the Holy Spirit, *St Theresa the Little Flower*. Translated by Magaret M. Repton, (Boston, Pauline Media, 1981) Page 265.

[67] *Ibid.* Page 265 & 266.

[68] *Ibid.* Page 266.

[69] These prayers were copied from various holy cards.

[70] Frances Parkinson Keyes, *Thérèse: Saint of a Little Way*, Page 175 & 176.

A world of Catholic reading
at your fingertips ...

CTS

... now online
Browse 500 titles at

www.cts-online.org.uk

Catholic Faith, Life, and Truth for all